סדר שלישי
The Third Seder
A Haggadah for Yom HaShoah

סדר שלישי
The Third Seder
A Haggadah for Yom HaShoah

Irene Lilienheim Angelico
and Yehudi Lindeman

Véhicule Press

Published with the generous assistance of the Canada Book Fund
of the Department of Canadian Heritage, the Jewish Community Foundation of Montreal,
the Tauben Family Foundation, and the Jack Dym Family Foundation.

In Memory of Leon and Irene Gutherz

All efforts have been made to ensure that all material is properly credited,
however, the publisher is pleased to respect any unacknowledged property rights.

A portion of the proceeds from the sale of this book
will be contributed to Survivors' causes and Holocaust education.

Artwork and design: J.W. Stewart
(www.jwstewart.net)
Calligraphy (pages 17 & 55): Susan Leviton
(www.susanlevitonarts.com)
Music notations: Tom Mennier
Special assistance: William Brooks
Printed by Marquis Printing Inc.

LIBRARY AND ARCHIVES CANADA CATALOGUING IN PUBLICATION

Angelico, Irene
The Third Seder : a Haggadah for Yom HaShoah / by Irene Lilienheim
Angelico and Yehudi Lindeman.
Accompanied by a CD with songs for Yom HaShoah
in English, Hebrew and Yiddish.

ISBN 978-1-55065-289-5 (book). – ISBN 978-1-55065-285-7 (book and CD)

1. Holocaust Remembrance Day. 2. Holocaust Remembrance Day--Prayers
and devotions. 3. Judaism--Prayers and devotions.

I. Lindeman, Yehudi II. Title.
BM675.H55A54 2010   296.4'39   C2010-900782-4

Published by Véhicule Press, Montréal, Québec, Canada
www.vehiculepress.com

Distribution in Canada by LitDistCo
www.litdistco.ca

Distributed in the U.S. by Independent Publishers Group
www.ipgbook.com

Printed in Canada on 100% post-consumer recycled paper.

*For our parents
and our children*

CONTENTS

FOREWORD

Mixing Memory with Desire

Rabbi Arthur Waskow

For Jews, history is not merely a record of what happened; it always points toward the future and, even more important, the present.

The archetypal case is the Torah's treatment of the "history" of the Exodus. Inextricably intertwined with the description of the transformative night of liberation are instructions for how to remember it. The text seems to be teaching that if Pharaoh fell in the forest — or in the Red Sea — but no one told the story, it would never have happened. The Passover Seder emerges in order to keep not just remembering but recreating liberation.

So it is in profound response to this wisdom that Jews would not only write histories about the Shoah, not only tell personal and family stories about it, but turn those memories into ritual — indeed, a Seder.

And here we are.

Of course, there is a problem. The Passover Seder remembers and recreates a great victory — not only for ancient Israel or for the continuing Jewish people, but for humanity at large: the victory of freedom, the victory of the God Whose Name is "I Will Be Who I Will Be" the God Who makes it real that the universe is open, is becoming, is indeed free.

But the Shoah is not only a disaster for the Jewish people but for that vision of a universe unfolding, always moving — though slowly — on that arc that bends toward justice.

So there is a great danger that by making memory of the Shoah into a ritual, we might lock ourselves into that world. The world of the God Who turns away, Who permits sheer force and violence to drown the hope of freedom. Instead of using ritual to transcend our trauma, we might lock ourselves into a post-traumatic stress, reenact the Holocaust instead of healing ourselves from it.

There are two ways to go beyond this danger. One is to look beyond our own pain, turn our own pain into a pointer toward the deadly dangers that afflict all peoples and indeed, in our epoch, all the web of life upon our planet. Then we can become teachers, not victims. And the willingness to teach is itself a victory.

The second path is to celebrate life after staring death in the face. Look hard into the bloody, blazing face of that Red Heifer, and then blink. See in the blinking the field of green that appears — green growing life.

Sing, dance, laugh, eat, share, love. No merely political triumph is enough to encode that kind of life-filled victory.

Those two paths of transformation are what a Seder for the Shoah needs to do — and this one, *The Third Seder*, beckons us into the doing.

INTRODUCTION

How is This Seder Different from All Other Seders?

For over two thousand years during Passover, each generation of Jews has told the story of our liberation from slavery in Egypt, passing it down from one generation to the next. We have never forgotten this ritual, and we have always been free to renew the telling for our time. After the Holocaust, as Elie Wiesel has said, we need to create something new — new symbols and new rituals to help us cope, understand and remember.

The Third Seder commemorates our liberation from the Holocaust, echoing Passover's celebration of liberation. For Survivors who were in camps, in hiding or on the run, the spring of 1945 was also the time of their liberation — our liberation.

In 1951 the Israeli Knesset inaugurated Yom HaShoah as Holocaust Remembrance Day and set the date as the 27th day of Nissan on the Jewish calendar. Since the 1960s, Jewish communities have observed Yom HaShoah worldwide, most often in large public events.

Many Jewish individuals and groups have been looking for ways to commemorate together in a more intimate setting. *The Third Seder: A Haggadah for Yom HaShoah* is our contribution. It is meant to be used at home with family and friends, or in schools, congregations and smaller community gatherings.

Our Haggadah is egalitarian, presuming an equal place for women and men. It is also inclusive. Recently, Christian and interfaith groups have also called for Yom HaShoah observance. We welcome them, as well as other religious and national groups, to use this Haggadah. In this Seder we have included places to reflect on present-day oppression and intolerance, and to acknowledge the suffering of others.

Seder means literally the order of things. This Seder for Yom HaShoah is organized around the Four Cups. The First Cup is to spring, the season of rebirth and new beginnings. The Second Cup is to freedom for our people. The Third Cup is to all our loved ones who died in the ghettos and forests and concentration camps, and to all the Survivors who have healed us with the strength and hope with which they rebuilt their lives. The Fourth Cup is to love and peace for all humanity.

We have created new symbols and rituals for The Third Seder. These include six candles and six yellow tulips for the six million Jews who were killed in the Holocaust, a flowering branch to represent Jewish life before the war and the continuity with Jewish life today, and seeds to represent rebirth. Unlike Passover, we only display the matzah at this Seder, and eat coarse bread instead, because most Jews commemorating Passover during the Holocaust did not have matzah to eat. At the heart of the Seder we dim the lights and each participant passes a flame of hope to their neighbor, until every candle in the group is lit. The person who receives the consummation of everyone's flame lights the six candles for the six million Jews who died in the Holocaust. Then we sing "Ani ma'amin" and say Kaddish for all those who died, many of whom have no one left to say Kaddish for them.

Since the time of King David, songs have occupied a central place in Jewish rituals. So it is with this Seder. Many of the songs are in Hebrew. Others are in Yiddish. Of the English songs, some come from the spiritual and folk tradition, and a few are original creations.

This Haggadah for Yom HaShoah reflects the new social and spiritual realities facing the Jewish people. It is inspired by those who died and those who survived, and by their many expressions of courage and resistance — from teaching Torah and mathematics in secret, from writing poems and songs of resistance, to rising up in the Warsaw ghetto, the forests near Vilna, and many other places throughout occupied Europe. It also reflects the beginning of a Jewish awakening in the aftermath of the Holocaust derived from a longing for renewal and tikkun olam.

We hope that The Third Seder will find its place within our Jewish tradition, to live on for generations, so that we will never forget and so that a Holocaust will never happen again.

HOW TO USE THIS HAGGADAH

Hold The Third Seder, ideally, on Yom HaShoah, the 27th day of Nissan on the Jewish calendar, or on the first Sunday following. Yom HaShoah is always in spring, the season of rebirth and renewal.

Share the Seder in a group around the family table, with your congregation or at a community gathering. To respect those we are remembering, forgo having a meal during this Seder, but serve bowls of nuts, seeds and dried fruits instead.

We suggest having a host and hostess lead the Seder. Start with In the Beginning and wait till after the blessing over the First Cup to welcome the participants and introduce *The Third Seder*. If you have a large group, you may want someone to pass a microphone from one reader to the next. Ask each participant to read a new passage in turn, as we do at Passover.

 Each new passage is marked with a blue leaf.

 Each new song is marked with a green leaf.

It takes about two hours to complete a relaxed Seder using this Haggadah. You may choose to shorten the Seder by leaving out certain passages. Encourage all the participants to tell stories and share their thoughts throughout the Seder. If you are privileged to have Survivors present, ask them especially to speak, perhaps giving them time to prepare beforehand. Their stories are the heart of this Seder for Yom HaShoah.

For the four cups, ask everyone to raise their cups and ask one participant to bless each one. If possible, ask a Survivor to bless the first cup and a son or daughter of Survivors to bless the second. Then everyone drinks. The essential rituals of the Seder are listed in the Order. The items you need for the Seder can be found in the Seder List.

We have included printed musical scores in the Appendix. Some editions of *The Third Seder* include a CD with recordings of all the songs. You have the choice of playing the music live at your Third Seder, or singing along with the CD. We hope the songs are so contagious that you sing them again and again, even after the Seder.

Over the years we have refined the Haggadah by adding some texts and songs and removing others. It remains a work in progress. You and your community may want to add materials of your own to the Haggadah for your personal use.

Some parts of the Seder may change in time. The prayer for each community that suffers should be updated to reflect what is happening in the world at the time of the Seder. We hope that one day there will be no communities that need to be named.

SEDER LIST

At the front:
A small table with 6 Yahrzeit candles and candleholders
A piano or keyboard (if possible)

At the head table:
2 holiday candles and candleholders
Water basin with cup and towel
Elijah and Miriam's cups

At each table:
A Haggadah for each guest
A small candle and candleholder for each guest
6 yellow tulips in a vase
A flowering branch
3 matzot on a plate
A loaf of dark bread
Bowls filled with seeds, such as sunflower and pomegranate
Nuts and nibbles
Wine and juice
Bread knife
Matches
Wine glasses, plates, silverware and napkins

ORDER

We light the Seder candles
We wash hands
We raise the cup to spring
We sing (throughout the Seder)
We raise the cup to freedom
We raise the matzah, but do not eat it
We speak about the oppression of Jews and non-Jews today
We eat the bread
We speak about the new symbols and rituals for Yom HaShoah
We raise the cup to those who died and to those who survived
We sing the Hymn of the Partisans
We dim the lights and tell the story
We pass the flame of hope from one to another
We sing "Ani Ma'amin"
We light six candles
We say Kaddish
We tell stories about the liberation
We hear the response of the next generations
We raise the cup to love and peace for all humanity
We dance
We sing Hatikvah

IN THE BEGINNING

Hostess:

In the beginning there was the Holocaust. We must therefore start all over again. We must write a new Talmud, just as we did after the destruction of the Second Temple. We did so then in order to accentuate the new beginning: until then we lived one way; from then on we had to undergo changes.

– Elie Wiesel

בְּכָל דּוֹר וָדוֹר
חַיָּב אָדָם
לִרְאוֹת
אֶת עַצְמוֹ
כְּאִלּוּ הוּא יָצָא
מִמִּצְרַיִם

Host:

Our first celebration of freedom took place over 3,000 years ago when the People of Israel liberated themselves from oppression by the Egyptians.

Since then, in every generation, Jews have celebrated the Exodus at Passover as if each of us were personally liberated from Egypt. We say to our children, as the Torah tells us, "It is because of what God did for me when I came forth from Egypt."

And so on Yom HaShoah, our generation and all our children to come will commemorate the liberation from the Holocaust as if we were each Survivors.

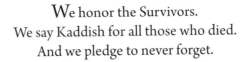
We honor the Survivors.
We say Kaddish for all those who died.
And we pledge to never forget.

Hostess:

Please join us in these blessings as we light the candles for the Third Seder.

The hostess lights the candles.

Baruch atah adonai, elohenu melech ha'olam,
shehechiyanu vekimanu, vehigiyanu lazman hazeh.

בָּרוּךְ אַתָּה יְיָ אֱלֹהֵינוּ מֶלֶךְ הָעוֹלָם.
שֶׁהֶחֱיָנוּ וְקִיְּמָנוּ וְהִגִּיעָנוּ לַזְּמַן הַזֶּה.

The month of spring — the first month, says the Torah: time to begin. As the flowers rise up against winter, so together we celebrate the freedom of new births and new beginnings.

– Rabbi Arthur Waskow

THE FIRST CUP

We raise this cup to spring, the season of new beginnings.

Baruch atah adonai, eloheinu melech ha'olam,
boreh pri hagafen.

בָּרוּךְ אַתָּה יְיָ אֱלֹהֵינוּ מֶלֶךְ הָעוֹלָם,
בּוֹרֵא פְּרִי הַגָּפֶן.

The host and hostess introduce The Third Seder and the participants, and talk about why this group has come together. Ask each person to read a short passage in turn. Everyone is encouraged to tell stories or personal accounts at any time.

HINEH MA TOV

הִנֵּה מַה טוֹב

Hineh ma tov uma na'im shevet achim gam yachad.	*2 times*	2 פעמים {	הִנֵּה מַה טוֹב וּמַה נָעִים שֶׁבֶת אָחִים גַּם יָחַד.	
Hineh ma tov, hineh ma tov Lalala. Lalala. Lalala.	*2 times*	2 פעמים {	הִנֵּה מַה טוֹב. הִנֵּה מַה טוֹב. לְהֲלֲהֲלֲה. לְהֲלֲהֲלֲה.	

How good and wonderful it is to sit together as brothers and sisters!

– Traditional, lyrics from Psalms 133:1

For lo, the winter is past
The rain is over and gone
The earth blossoms forth in flowers
And the song of the birds is heard
The fig tree puts forth her green figs
Our vineyards are heavy with grapes
Let us arise, for it is Spring
Let us go forth into the fields

Let us lodge in the villages
Let us get up early to the vineyards
Let us see if the vines flourish
Whether the tender grapes appear
And the pomegranates burst forth
And at our gates
Are all manner of pleasant fruits.

— Adapted from The Song of Songs 2:11-13

ERETZ ZAVAT CHALAV UD'VASH

אֶרֶץ זָבַת חָלָב וּדְבָשׁ

Eretz zavat chalav, chalav ud'vash   } 4 times

Eretz zavat chalav, zavat chalav ud'vash } 2 times

4{ פעמים אֶרֶץ זָבַת חָלָב. חָלָב וּדְבָשׁ

2{ פעמים סאֶרֶץ זָבַת חָלָב. זָבַת חָלָב וּדְבָשׁ.

A land flowing with milk and honey

— Traditional, lyrics from Exodus 3:8

For many peoples, spring is a time of celebration, a festival of rebirth when the earth is fertile and we plant seeds to bring forth flowers and food.

For Jews, spring is also the time we celebrate our rebirth as a people, in our liberation during the Exodus from Egypt, in our liberation from the Holocaust in Europe.

If the son or daughter of a Survivor is present
the hostess invites them to raise the second cup.

THE SECOND CUP

We raise this cup to our liberation from Egypt and our rebirth as a people.

Baruch atah adonai, eloheinu melech ha'olam,
boreh pri hagafen.

בָּרוּךְ אַתָּה יְיָ אֱלֹהֵינוּ מֶלֶךְ הָעוֹלָם,
בּוֹרֵא פְּרִי הַגָּפֶן.

"Remember the time when you were a slave in Egypt" is one of the most haunting refrains of our collective memory. Moses, the first great man with whom the people identify, is first and foremost a liberator. All Jewish history — the image Jews have forged of themselves — is constructed or reconstructed in this perspective: Oppression — Liberation."

– Albert Memmi

The host holds up the matzah, saying:

This is the bread of affliction that our ancestors ate in the land of Egypt.
Let all who are hungry come and eat it with us.
Let all who have nowhere to go come and share with us.
This year we are in Galut.
Next year, may we find our way to Israel.
This year we are oppressed people.
Next year, may we be truly liberated!

– Passover Haggadah

Miriam was a prophetess who saved the life of her baby brother Moses. After he led the Israelites in the Exodus from Pharaoh's land, Miriam led the women in an joyful dance to celebrate their freedom.

MIRIAM

They danced, they danced, oh how they danced,
they danced the night away.
Clapped their hands and stamped their feet
with voices loud they praised.

They danced with joy, they danced with grace,
they danced on nimble feet,
kicked up their heels, threw back their heads,
hypnotic with the beat.

And Miriam took her timbrel out
and all the women danced. } *2 times*
Vatikach Miriam ha neviyah et hatof beyadah
vateitzena kol hanashim achareiyah.

They danced so hard, they danced so fast,
they danced with movement strong,
laughed and cried, brought out alive,
they danced until the dawn.

Some carrying child, some baking bread,
Weeping as they prayed,
But when they heard that music start
They put their pain away.

And Miriam took her timbrel out
and all the women danced. } *2 times*
Vatikach Miriam ha neviyah et hatof beyadah
vateitzena kol hanashim achareiyah.

– Music and lyrics by G. Rayzel Robinson Raphael

The holiday of Passover has often been synonymous with danger; especially for the Jews of Spain and Portugal following the expulsion.

ZOG MARAN

זאָג מאַראַן

Zog Maran, du bruder mayner,
vu is greyt der Seyder dayner?
In tifer heyl, in a cheyder,
dort hob ich gegreyt mayn Seyder. } 2 times

פעמים 2 {
זאָג מאַראַן. דו ברודער מיַינער,
וואו איז גרייט דער סדר דיַינער?
-- אין טיפער הייל. אין אַ חדר.
דאָרט האָב איך גענגרייט מיַין סדר.

Zog Maran, mir vu, bay vemen
vestu vayse matses nemen?
In der heyl, oyf Gots barotn,
hot mayn vayb dem teyg geknotn. } 2 times

פעמים 2 {
זאָג מאַראַן. מיר וואו. ביַי וועמען
וועסטו וויַיסע מצות נעמען?
-- אין דער הייל. אויף גאָטס באַראָטן
האָט מיַין וויַיב דעם טייג געקנאָטן.

Zog Maran, vi vest zich klign
a Hagode vu tsu krign?
In der heyl, in tife shpaltn
hob ich zi shoyn lang behaltn. } 2 times

פעמים 2 {
זאָג מאַראַן, ווי וועסט זיך קליגן
אַ הגדה וואו צו קריגן?
-- אין דער הייל. אין טיפע שפּאַלטן
האָב איך זי שוין לאַנג באַהאַלטן.

Zog Maran, vi vest zich vern
ven men vet dayn kol derhern?
Ven der soyne vet mich fangen,
vel ich shtarbn mit gezangen. } 2 times

פעמים 2 {
זאָג מאַראַן, ווי וועסט זיך ווערן
ווען מען וועט דיַין קול דערהערן?
-- ווען דער שׂונא וועט מיך פֿאַנגען.
וועל איך שטאַרבן מיט געזאַנגען.

Tell me Marrano, my brother
where have you prepared your Seder?
In a room in a deep cellar
there is my Seder ready.

Tell me Marrano, from whom
will you get white matzot?
In the cellar under God's protection
my wife kneaded the dough.

Tell me Marrano, how will you
manage to get a Haggadah?
In the cellar, in a deep crevice
I hid a Haggadah long ago.

Tell me Marrano, if your voice will be heard
what will you do?
When the enemy captures me
I will die singing.

– Music by Shmuel Bugatch, lyrics by Avrom Reisen

Over time, the story of Jewish slavery and liberation has been adopted by many other people enslaved and seeking freedom, as in this Afro-American spiritual.

Sing the song slowly one time, then fast:

GO DOWN MOSES

When Israel was in Egypt's land.
Let my people go.
Oppressed so hard they could not stand
Let my people go

Go down Moses
Way down in Egypt's land.
Tell ole Pharaoh
To let my people go.

Tonight we gather to remember.

We remember our Exodus from Egypt, when we broke our bonds of slavery and, with God's help, returned to Eretz Israel.

We remember that on the night of the first Seder we broke our bonds of fear, led by the fire in the souls of the heroes of the Warsaw Ghetto.

We remember that we are a people of freedom, a nation that bows only to God.

We remember that although those of us around this Seder table are free, we are not all free; that many of us still struggle against those who would have us deny our faith, our homeland and our heritage.

> – Anti-Defamation League

> *Together:*

With each community that suffers our cup of joy is lessened:
Armenia, Rwanda, Somalia, Sudan, Bosnia, Cambodia, Burma, Tibet and aboriginal peoples around the world.

May we all soon be safe.

> *Participants may want to name and discuss any country or community endangered by religious, ethnic or racial intolerance today.*

Our Seder is an invitation to all of us, in our own sanctuary — the sanctuary of home, or synagogue, or country — to work together to provide sanctuary to all those who are now uprooted and homeless, fleeing oppression.

If I am not for myself, who will be for me?
But if I am only for myself, what am I?
And if not now, when?

> – Rabbi Hillel, Pirkei Avot 1:14

> *The hostess holds up each symbol as she describes its new meaning for Yom HaShoah.*

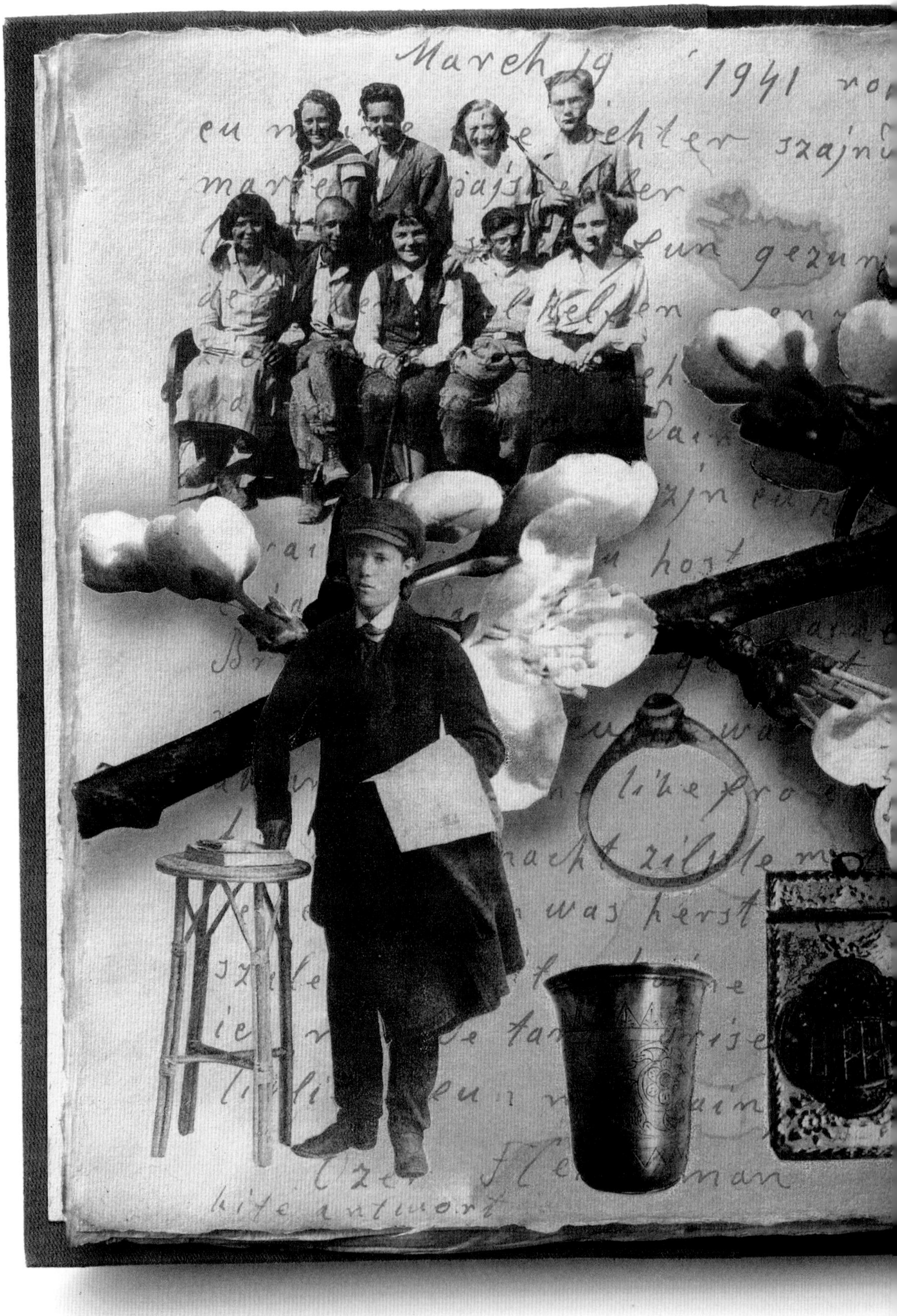
March 19 1941

Tonight we are creating new symbols and rituals to help us remember our liberation from the Holocaust. Our new rituals echo those of Passover, the commemoration of our first liberation. They are chosen to recall the suffering and hope of the darkest nights in the camps, and the mixed joy and pain of the liberation. They remind us of life before the war, and of our rebirth after the liberation. Because of the solemnity of this occasion, we do not share a meal at our Seder.

We choose this flowering branch to remind us of the vibrant Jewish life that thrived everywhere before the war. We have lost that world forever. But although a branch of our heritage has been broken off, the tree of generations of Jewish life is still strong and will grow forever.

The six yellow tulips are for the six million Jewish men, women and children who died in the Holocaust. Part of us died with them. We choose flowers to represent them because flowers remind us of their beauty, and because so many were only in the blossom of their youth. We choose tulips because they remind us of the people of Holland, along with the people of Poland and Righteous Gentiles everywhere, who risked their own lives to save Jews in the Holocaust. We choose yellow to show pride in the yellow star most Jews were forced to wear.

We choose these seeds to represent rebirth. The Survivors rebuilt their lives with love and hope, even after the Holocaust. The birthrate in the DP camps after the liberation was the highest ever known to humankind. Survivors taught their children, and all the generations to follow, the strength of the will to life. They fought for the State of Israel, where we were reborn as a nation. In our old/new country they planted seeds and brought life to the desert.

– Irene Lilienheim Angelico

Today we are free to celebrate our liberation from Egypt. At Passover, we eat matzah to remind us of the haste with which we fled Egypt. But in Bergen-Belsen in 1944, there was no matzah to eat. Rather than allow the inmates to endanger their lives by foregoing their main source of sustenance, the rabbis decreed that they could eat bread, provided they recite the following prayer:

It is our desire to do Your will and to celebrate the festival of Passover by eating matzah and observing the prohibition of leavened food. But our heart is pained that the enslavement prevents us for we are in danger of our lives. Behold, we are prepared and ready to fulfill Your commandment: "You shall live by my commandments and not die by them." And we pray to You that You may keep us alive and preserve us and redeem us speedily so that we may observe Your statutes and do Your will and serve You with a perfect heart. Amen.

> – Rabbis in the Bergen-Belsen concentration camp

The host cuts the bread, and passes a piece of bread to everyone present, explaining the new ritual:

Tonight at our Third Seder for Yom HaShoah, although we are privileged to have matzah, we will eat only chametz to remind us of the bodily and spiritual deprivation our loved ones suffered during the Holocaust.

Baruch atah adonai, eloheinu melech h'olam, hamotzi lechem min ha'aretz.

בָּרוּךְ אַתָּה יְיָ אֱלֹהֵינוּ מֶלֶךְ הָעוֹלָם. הַמּוֹצִיא לֶחֶם מִן הָאָרֶץ.

Everyone eats the bread.

THE THIRD CUP

We raise this cup to all our loved ones who died in the ghettos and forests and concentration camps, and to all the Survivors who have healed us with the strength and hope with which they rebuilt our lives.

Baruch atah adonai, eloheinu melech ha'olam, boreh pri hagafen.

בָּרוּךְ אַתָּה יְיָ אֱלֹהֵינוּ מֶלֶךְ הָעוֹלָם. בּוֹרֵא פְּרִי הַגָּפֶן.

When Rabbi Meir died, there were no more makers of parables. When Ben Zoma died, there were no more expounders. When Rabbi Joshua died, goodness departed from this world. When Rabbi Shimon ben Gamaliel died, the locusts came and troubles grew. When Rabbi Eleazar ben Azariah died, wealth departed from the sages. When Rabbi Akiba died, the glory of the Law ceased.

– Mishna Sota 9:15, translated by Herbert Danby

When Kalman the shoemaker died, there were no more craftsmen. When Basha the musician died, artistry departed from this world. When Jonah the wagon driver went up in smoke, the road washed away and troubles grew. When Rivka the orphan died, goodness departed from this world.

– David Roskies, adapted by the editors

SHOAH

PASSOVER, 1942

As Jews once more observe the annual celebration of the Passover, we cannot but draw the inevitable parallel between its plight in Europe today and the plight of its ancestors under the Egyptian bondage. For he who surveys that unhappy continent, now converted into a prison and a slaughterhouse, must be impressed by the fact that the tyrant of today has actually out-Pharaoh-ed Pharaoh. Where the Egyptian despot sought to destroy every Jewish son that was born, the Nazi barbarian has set as his aim the complete and total annihilation of our people; and where he of yore used simple methods to encompass his ends, the twentieth-century führer has availed himself of all the techniques of science and organization to achieve his plan of concentrated and scheduled murder.

Every cruelty that a madman could invent against us, the insane fury of the Reich has invented. In the torture houses of the concentration camps, our brothers and sisters fall in their hundreds; before the common graves of the mass-execution, they perish in their thousands; in their tens of thousands they fall victim to the famine and pestilence of the ghetto. The gas chamber, the firing squad – it is with these that Hitler is taking a grim census of our people.

– Samuel Bronfman

Together:

Count by ones to six million, a number each second. 1, 2, 3, 4, 5, 6, 7 … you will be here all April, all May, all June and all July … 8, 9, 10, 11, 12 … not even naming names, each person a number … 13, 14, 15, 16, 17, 18, 19, 20, 21, 22 … The Germans always started over again at 200,000 … 23, 24, 25, 26, 27, 28, 29, 30, 31, 32, 33 ….

In the fall of 1941, the Germans marched the Jews of Kiev to a nearby ravine known as Babi Yar, then opened fire on all 33,000 men, women and children. The ravine became their grave. Years later, a Russian gentile wrote this poem, which became known around the world.

BABI YAR

No gravestone stands on Babi Yar,
only coarse earth heaped roughly
    on the gash
Such dread comes over me. I feel so old,
old as the Jews. Today, I am a Jew.
Now I go wandering, an Egyptian slave,
and now I perish, splayed upon the cross.

I am each old man slaughtered,
    each child shot.
The marks of nails are still upon my flesh.
And I am Dreyfus whom the gentry hound:
And I am behind the bars, caught in a ring,
belied, denounced, and spat upon I stand,
while dainty ladies in their lacy frills
squealing, poke parasols into my face.

I am that little boy in Bialystok,
whose blood flows, spreading darkly on the
    floor.
The rowdy lords of the saloon make sport,
reeking alike of vodka and of leek.
Booted aside, weak, helpless, I, the child
who begs in vain while the pogromchik mob
guffaws and shouts:
    "Save Russia, beat the Jews!"
The shopman's blows fall
    on my mother's back.

Now, in this moment, I am Anne Frank,
frail and transparent as an April twig.

   – Yevgeny Yevtushenko

I love as she; I need no ready phrases.
Only to look into each other's eyes!
How little we can sense, how little see.
Leaves are forbidden us, the sky forbidden.

Yet how much still remains;
    how strangely sweet
to hold each other close in the dark room.
They come? No, do not fear.
    These are the gales
of spring: she bursts into this gloom.
Come to me: quickly, let me kiss your lips.
They break the door?
    No, no, the ice is breaking.

On Babi Yar weeds rustle. The tall trees
like judges loom and threaten.
All screams in silence. I take off my cap
and I feel that I am slowly turning gray.
And I too have become a soundless cry
over the thousands that lie buried here.
None of me will forget.

Let the glad "Internationale" blare forth,
when earth's last anti-Semite lies in earth.
No drop of Jewish blood flows in my veins,
but anti-Semites with a dull, gnarled hate
detest me like a Jew.
O know me truly Russian
through their hate!

The continuing slaughter of Jewish communities led to greater armed resistance among the Jews. The song "Shtil di nacht" is about the bravery of one woman, Vitka Kempner, who bravely fought with the partisans in the Rudninkai Forest near Vilna.

SHTIL DI NACHT

שטיל די נאַכט

Shtil di nacht iz oysgeshternt
un der frost hot shtark gebrent,
tsi gedenkstu, vi ich hob dich gelernt
haltn a shpayer in di hent?

שטיל די נאַכט איז אויסגעשטערנט
און דער פראָסט האָט שטאַרק געברענט.
צי געדענקסטו. ווי איך האָב דיך געלערנט
האַלטן אַ שפּייער אין די הענט?

A moyd, a peltsl un a beret
un halt in hant fest a nagan,
a moyd mit a sametenem ponim
hit op dem soynes karavan.

אַ מויד. אַ פּעלצל און אַ בערעט
און האַלט אין האַנט פעסט אַ נאַגאַן.
אַ מויד מיט אַ סאַמעטענעם פּנים
היט אָפ דעם שונאס קאַראַוואַן.

Getsilt, geshosn un getrofn
hot ir kleyninker pistoyl,
an oito a fulinken mit vof'n
farhaltn hot zi mit eyn koyl.

געצילט. געשאָסן און געטראָפן
האָט איר קליינינקער פּיסטויל.
אַן אויטאָ אַ פולינקן מיט וואָפן
פאַרהאַלטן האָט זי מיט איין קויל.

Fartog, fun vald aroysgekroch'n,
mit shney-girlandn oyf di hor,
gemutikt fun kleyninkn nitsoch'n,
far undzer nayem, frayen dor!

פאַרטאָג. פון וואַלד אַרויסגעקראָכן.
מיט שניי-גירלאַנדן אויף די האָר.
געמוטיקט פון קליינינקן נצחון.
פאַר אונדזער נייעם. פרייען דור!

The night is still and bright with stars,
there is a burning frost.
Do you remember I showed you
how to hold a gun in your hand?

A girl in a fur jacket and a beret,
a pistol gripped tightly in her hand,
a girl with a face smooth as velvet
holds up the enemy convoy.

She aims, fires and shoots her target.
With a bullet from her small gun
she stops and seizes
a truck full of arms.

At daybreak she steals from the forest,
a garland of snow in her hair,
proud of the little victory she won
for our new and free generation!

– Music and lyrics by Hirsh Glik, translated by Yehudi Lindeman

WARSAW

On April 19, 1943, the first night of Passover, the Jews of the Warsaw Ghetto rose up. They were hungry and weak, outnumbered and under-armed. The Nazis had surrounded the ghetto with their tanks and guns and expected to finish the job quickly. But for forty-three days and nights the Warsaw Jews fought for their dignity and for the dignity of all human life.

Dearest Bronia,

My hand trembles, I cannot write. We fare terribly. Our moments are numbered. God alone knows if we'll ever see you again. I write and cry, my children despair — one wants so much to stay alive. All of us say good-bye to all of you. I am not in contact with Hania and Hala, so you, my Bronia, write to them and say good-bye from us. We kiss you. Write immediately. Perhaps I shall still receive your letter. If you do not hear from me soon, then we are probably no longer alive.

> – Letters from the Ghetto

When news of the uprising reached Hirsh Glik, it inspired him to write "Zog nit keyn mol". His song spread through Vilna, then to other ghettos, generating a renewed sense of pride and will.

Stand to sing the Hymn of the Partisans:

זאָג ניט קיין מאָל

זאָג ניט קיין מאָל, אַז דו גייסט דעם לעצטן וועג,
כאָטש הימלען בלייענע פֿאַרשטעלן בלויע טעג.
קומען וועט נאָך אונדזער אויסגעבענקטע שעה,
ס׳וועט אַ פויק טאָן אונדזער טראָט: "מיר זײַנען דאָ!"

פֿון גרינעם פּאַלמענלאַנד ביז ווײַסן לאַנד פֿון שניי,
מיר קומען אָן מיט אונדזער פּיין, מיט אונדזער וויי.
און ווּ געפֿאַלן ס׳איז אַ שפּריץ פֿון אונדזער בלוט,
שפּראָצן וועט דאָרט אונדזער גבֿורה, אונדזער מוט.

ס׳וועט די מאָרגנזון באַגילדן אַ ונדז דעם הײַנט,
און דער נעכטן וועט פֿאַרשווינדן מיטן פֿײַנד.
נאָר אויב פֿאַרזאַמען וועט די זון און דער קאַיאָר,
ווי אַ פּאַראָל זאָל גיין דאָס ליד פֿון דור צו דור!

געשריבן איז דאָס ליד מיט בלוט און ניט מיט בלײַ,
ס׳איז ניט קיין לידל פֿון אַ פֿויגל אויף דער פֿרײַ –
דאָס האָט אַ פֿאָלק צעווישן פֿאַלנדיקע ווענט
דאָס ליד געזונגען מיט נאַגאַנעס אין די הענט.

טאָ זאָג ניט ניט קיין מאָל, אַז דו גייסט דעם לעצטן וועג,
כאָטש הימלען בלײַענע פֿאַרשטעלן בלאָע טעג.
קומען וועט נאָך אונדזער אויסגעבענקטע שעה,
ס׳וועט אַ פויק טאָן אונדזער טראָט: "מיר זײַנען דאָ!"

ZOG NIT KEYN MOL

Zog nit keyn mol, az du geyst dem letstn veg,
chotsh himlen blayene farshteln bloye teg.
Kumen vet noch undzer oysgebenkte sho,
s'vet a poyk ton undzer trot: "mir zaynen do!"

Fun grinem palmenland biz vaysn land fun shney,
mir kumen on mit undzer payn, mit undzer vey.
Un vu gefaln s'iz a shprits fun undzer blut,
shprotsen vet dort undzer gvure, undzer mut.

S'vet di morgenzun bagildn undz dem haynt,
un der nechtn vet farshvindn mitn faynd.
Nor ob farzamen vet di zun an der kayor,
vi a parol zol geyn dos lid fun dor tsu dor!

Geshribn iz dos lid mit blut un nit mit blay,
s'iz nit keyn lidl fun a foygl oyf der fray -
dos hot a folk ts'vishn falndike vent
dos lid gezungen mit naganes in di hent.

To zog nit keyn mol, az du geyst dem letstn veg,
chotsh himlen blayene farshteln bloye teg.
Kumen vet noch undzer oysgebenkte sho,
s'vet a poyk ton undzer trot: "mir zaynen do!"

Never say that you are going your last way,
though lead-filled skies above blot out the blue of day.
The hour for which we long will certainly appear,
the earth shall thunder 'neath our tread that: "we are here!"

From lands of green palm trees to lands all white with snow,
we are coming with our pain, with our woe.
And where'er a spurt of our blood did drop,
our courage will again sprout from that spot.

For us the morning sun will radiate the day,
and the enemy and past will fade away.
But should the dawn delay or sunrise wait too long,
then let all future generations sing this song!

This song was written with our blood and not with lead,
this is no song of free birds flying overhead —
but a people amid crumbling walls did stand
they stood and sang this song with rifles held in hand.

Never say that you are going your last way,
though lead-filled skies above blot out the blue of day.
The hour for which we long will certainly appear,
the earth shall thunder 'neath our tread that: "we are here!"

— Music and lyrics by Hirsh Glik, translated by Elliot Palevsky

Be seated.

AT MY BAR MITZVAH – AND HIS

Dedicated to the memory of a thirteen-year-old hero of the Resistance

When I was thirteen, I became Bar Mitzvah.
    When he was thirteen, he became Bar Mitzvah.

When I was thirteen, my teachers taught me — to put Tefillin on my arm.
    When he was thirteen, his teachers taught him — to throw a hand grenade with his arm.

When I was thirteen, I studied — the pathways of the Bible and roadways of the Talmud.
    When he was thirteen, he studied — the canals of Warsaw and the sewers of the Ghetto.

At my Bar Mitzvah, I took an oath to live as a Jew.
    At his Bar Mitzvah, he took an oath to die as a Jew.

At my Bar Mitzvah, I blessed God.
    At his Bar Mitzvah, he questioned God.

At my Bar Mitzvah, I lifted my voice and sang.
    At his Bar Mitzvah, he lifted his fists and fought.

At my Bar Mitzvah, I wore a new Tallit over a new suit.
    At his Bar Mitzvah, he wore a rifle and bullets over a suit of rags.

At my Bar Mitzvah, they praised my voice, my song, my melody.
    At his Bar Mitzvah, they praised his strength, his courage, his fearlessness.

When I was thirteen, I was called up to the Torah — I went to the Bimah.
    When he was thirteen, his body went up in smoke — his soul rose to God.

When I was thirteen, I became Bar Mitzvah — and lived.
    When he was thirteen, he became Bar Mitzvah — and lives now within each of us.

    – Rabbi Howard Kahn

FIRE AND ROSES

Little boys in dirty clothes were playing yesterday
eyes so full of light still look my way

How could they know what the future would hold
those little girls and boys had no chance to become old
If I could have saved those eyes from what they had to see
the calculated killing, cold-blooded cruelty.

The women hang their washing on the line
voices laughing, chattering like chimes

How I wish that I could reach back in time
across the fence of history with all I claim as mine
How I wish that when I tuck my child into bed
she could see their faces, hear their songs instead.

The men are strolling slowly down the street
they stop and chat with old friends that they meet

How I wish that I could reach back in time
to break bread together, drink a toast to the divine
How I wish that they could all gather with us here
tell the million stories lost when millions disappeared.

Their souls cry out so loudly to me
in the roaring raging flame of inhumanity

But I feed them roses, they taste my tears and smile
I will be their comfort for a little while
Yes, I feed them roses, I give them each a smile
I will be their comfort for awhile.

– Music and lyrics by Ruth Saphir and Cedric M. Speyer

It is true that nowhere on earth and never before in history could one experience the absurdity of existence as in the German ghettos and camps: but it is also true that nowhere else in the world and never before could one experience the nobility of existence as there and then.

– Eliezer Berkovits

Resistance took many forms among the countless heroes and heroines in the ghettos and camps: teachers giving classes by candlelight, even at the risk of death; writers publishing clandestine newspapers to inform their fellow Jews; mothers choosing to stay with their children to give them comfort in the last moments of their lives.

KOL HA'OLAM KULO

כָּל הָעוֹלָם כֻּלּוֹ

Kol ha'olam kulo
gesher tzar me'od } 3 times
kol ha'olam kulo
gesher tzar me'od } 2 times

כָּל הָעוֹלָם כֻּלּוֹ
גֶּשֶׁר צַר מְאֹד. 3 } פעמים
כָּל הָעוֹלָם כֻּלּוֹ
גֶּשֶׁר צַר מְאֹד 2 } פעמים

Veha'ikar, veha'ikar
lo lefached, lo lefached klal
veha'ikar, veha'ikar
lo lefached klal

וְהָעִיקָר. וְהָעִיקָר
לֹא לְפַחֵד. לֹא לְפַחֵד כְּלָל
וְהָעִיקָר. וְהָעִיקָר
לֹא לְפַחֵד כְּלָל.

All the world is
just a narrow bridge,
All the world is
just a narrow bridge.

But above all, but above all,
is not to fear, not to fear at all.
But above all, but above all,
is not to fear at all.

– Music by B. Chait, lyrics from Rabbi Nachman of Bratzlav

THE FIFTH CHILD

On Passover we speak of four children. On this night, we remember the fifth child. This is a child of the Shoah who did not survive to ask.

Therefore, we ask for that child — why?

We are like the simple child. We have no answer.

We answer that child's question with silence. In silence, we remember that dark time. In silence, we remember that Jews preserved their image of God in the struggle for life. In silence, we remember the Seder nights in the forests, ghettos, and camps; we remember that Seder night when the Warsaw Ghetto rose in revolt.

> – Rabbi Irving Greenberg

Dim the lights.

In silence, we light the flame of hope that survived through the darkest nights of the Holocaust.

Pass the flame, one to another, until everyone's candle is lit.

The last person lights six candles for the six million Jews who were killed in the Holocaust.

Everyone stand. We sing as the Jews of the Warsaw Ghetto did, when they were being led away:

ANI MA'AMIN   אֲנִי מַאֲמִין

Ani ma'amin, ani ma'amin,
ani ma'amin —
be'emuna shleyma
beviat hamashi'ach,
beviat hamashi'ach ani ma'amin.
Ve'af al pi she, yitmameyah
im kol zeh ani ma'amin.

אֲנִי מַאֲמִין, אֲנִי מַאֲמִין,
אֲנִי מַאֲמִין
בֶּאֱמוּנָה שְׁלֵמָה
בְּבִיאַת הַמָּשִׁיחַ.
בְּבִיאַת הַמָּשִׁיחַ אֲנִי מַאֲמִין.
וְאַף עַל פִּי שֶׁיִּתְמַהְמֵהַּ.
עִם כָּל-זֶה אֲנִי מַאֲמִין.

I believe
with complete faith
that the Mashiach will come.
And even though the Mashiach may tarry,
in spite of this, I still believe.

> – Traditional, lyrics from Maimonides

Remain standing.

It is our tradition to say Kaddish, a prayer of praise and peace, for a loved one who has died. During the Holocaust many died with no one to remember them. Tonight we remember.

Let us stand and read together. Call out any additional names you wish to remember.

Auschwitz, Babi Yar, Belzec, Bergen-Belsen, Buchenwald, Budapest, Chelmno, Dachau, Drancy, Gross-Rosen, Lida, Lodz, Lvov, Magdeburg, Majdanek, Mauthausen, Mechelen, Minsk, Neuengamme, Ravensbrück, Riga, Sachsenhausen, Salonika, Sobibor, Stutthof, Theresienstadt, Transnistria, Trawniki, Treblinka, Vilna, Warsaw, Westerbork

יִזְכּוֹר אֱלֹהִים נִשְׁמוֹת הַקְּדוֹשִׁים וְהַטְּהוֹרִים שֶׁנֶּהֶרְגוּ. שֶׁנִּשְׁחֲטוּ וְשֶׁנִּשְׂרְפוּ. וְשֶׁנִּטְבְּעוּ וְשֶׁנֶּחְנְקוּ עַל קְדוּשׁ הַשֵּׁם. בַּעֲבוּר שֶׁנּוֹדְרִים צְדָקָה בְּעַד הַזְכָּרַת נִשְׁמוֹתֵיהֶם. בִּשְׂכַר זֶה. תִּהְיֶינָה נַפְשׁוֹתֵיהֶם צְרוּרוֹת בִּצְרוֹר הַחַיִּים עִם נִשְׁמוֹת אַבְרָהָם יִצְחָק וְיַעֲקֹב. שָׂרָה רִבְקָה רָחֵל וְלֵאָה. וְעִם שְׁאָר צַדִּיקִים וְצִדְקָנִיּוֹת שֶׁבְּגַן עֵדֶן. וְנֹאמַר אָמֵן.

May God remember the holy and pure souls who have been slaughtered, burned, drowned or strangled for their loyalty to God. We pledge charity in their memory and pray that their souls be kept among the immortals souls of Abraham, Isaac, Jacob, Sarah, Rebeccah, Rachel, Leah, and all the righteous men and women in paradise; and let us say: Amen.

– Yizkor for Martyrs

Let us say Kaddish together

KADDISH

קַדִּישׁ

Yitgadal veyitkadash shmei rabah	יִתְגַּדַּל וְיִתְקַדַּשׁ שְׁמֵהּ רַבָּא.
be'almah dee vrah chirutay	בְּעָלְמָא דִּי בְרָא כִרְעוּתֵהּ
veyamlich malchutay	וְיַמְלִיךְ מַלְכוּתֵהּ.
bechayeichon uveyomeichon	בְּחַיֵּיכוֹן וּבְיוֹמֵיכוֹן
uvechayei dee chol beit yisrael	וּבְחַיֵּי דְכָל בֵּית יִשְׂרָאֵל.
be'agalah uvizman kariv	בַּעֲגָלָא וּבִזְמַן קָרִיב
ve'imru amen.	וְאִמְרוּ אָמֵן:
Yehei shmei rabah mevarach	יְהֵא שְׁמֵהּ רַבָּא מְבָרַךְ
le'alam ule'almei almaya.	לְעָלַם וּלְעָלְמֵי עָלְמַיָּא:
Yitbarach ve yishtabach	יִתְבָּרַךְ וְיִשְׁתַּבַּח
veyitpa'ar veyitromam veyitnaseh	וְיִתְפָּאַר וְיִתְרוֹמַם. וְיִתְנַשֵּׂא
veyithadar veyit'aleh veyithalal	וְיִתְהַדָּר וְיִתְעַלֶּה וְיִתְהַלָּל
shmei dee kudsha berich-hu.	שְׁמֵהּ דְּקֻדְשָׁא
Le'eilah u'le'eilah min kol birchatah	בְּרִיךְ הוּא לְעֵלָּא מִן כָּל בִּרְכָתָא
veshiratah tushbechatah venecheimatah	וְשִׁירָתָא תֻּשְׁבְּחָתָא וְנֶחֱמָתָא.
dee amiran be'almah	דַּאֲמִירָן בְּעָלְמָא.
ve'imru amen.	וְאִמְרוּ אָמֵן:
Yehei shlamah rabah min shemayah	יְהֵא שְׁלָמָא רַבָּא מִן שְׁמַיָּא
vechayim aleinu	וְחַיִּים טוֹבִים עָלֵינוּ
ve'al kol yisrael	וְעַל כָּל יִשְׂרָאֵל
ve'imru amen.	וְאִמְרוּ אָמֵן:
Oseh shalom bimromav	עוֹשֶׂה שָׁלוֹם בִּמְרוֹמָיו
Hu ya'aseh shalom aleinu	הוּא יַעֲשֶׂה שָׁלוֹם עָלֵינוּ
ve'al kol yisrael	וְעַל כָּל יִשְׂרָאֵל.
ve'al kol yoshvei tevel	וְעַל כָּל יוֹשְׁבֵי תֵבֵל.
ve'imru amen.	וְאִמְרוּ אָמֵן:

Turn the lights up and be seated.

The Legacy and The Acceptance were written for the World Gathering of Jewish Survivors, which took place in Jerusalem in 1981, thirty-six years after the war. Thousands of Survivors stood together at the Western Wall to deliver the Legacy to the next generation. Then their children stood to declare their acceptance in unison.

The host invites any Survivors who were there to describe the event and then invites all the Survivors present to stand and say the Oath:

THE LEGACY

WE TAKE THIS OATH! We take it in the shadow of flames whose tongues scar the soul of our people. We vow in the name of dead parents and children; we vow, with our sadness hidden, our faith renewed; we vow, we shall never let the sacred memory of our perished Six Million be scorned or erased.

WE SAW THEM hungry, in fear, we saw them rush to battle, we saw them in the loneliness of night – true to their faith. At the threshold of death, we saw them. We received their silence in silence, merged their tears with ours.

Deportations, executions, mass graves, death camps; mute prayers, cries of revolt, desperation, torn scrolls; cities and towns, villages and hamlets; the young, the old, the rich, the poor, ghetto fighters and partisans, scholars and messianic dreamers, ravaged faces, fists raised. Like clouds of fire, all have vanished.

WE TAKE THIS OATH! Vision becomes word, to be handed down from father to son, from mother to daughter, from generation to generation.

REMEMBER what the German killers and their accomplices did to our people. Remember them with rage and contempt. Remember what an indifferent world did to us and to itself. Remember the victims with pride and with sorrow. Remember also the deeds of the righteous Gentiles.

WE SHALL ALSO REMEMBER the miracle of the Jewish rebirth in the land of our ancestors, in the independent State of Israel. Here, pioneers and fighters returned to our people the dignity and majesty of nationhood. From the ruins of their lives, orphans and widows built homes and old-new fortresses on our redeemed land. To the end of our days we shall remember all those who realized and raised their dream — our dream — redemption to the loftiest heights.

WE TAKE THIS OATH here [as they did] in Jerusalem, our eternal spiritual sanctuary. Let our legacy endure as a stone of the Temple Wall. For here prayers and memories burn. They burn and burn and will not be consumed.

– Elie Wiesel, translated by Menachem Rosensaft

Be seated.

LIBERATION

LYDIA'S STORY

It was a gloomy morning and I had a feeling that something bad was going to happen. The Germans announced that we were marching to a new camp, but somebody came back to warn us that the Germans were taking everybody to the River Elbe to kill us. The river was already red with blood.

The Nazis were pushing and shouting. Some people were crying, some praying, others were resigned to their fate. When someone fell, the Nazis shot them. Finally, I decided it couldn't be far, so I grabbed Hanka's hand and whispered, "Run, now! Run."

When we ran, everyone started to run, all in different directions. The Germans came after us, shouting "*Verflucte Juden* (Dirty Jews)!" We heard a barrage of machine guns. People were falling all around. "Don't look back," I cried.

We ran past bombed buildings, dodging piles of rubble. Finally, I saw a sign that said "Laundry" and we ran down the stairs. We hid behind two huge washing kettles, listening to the shouting and machine guns, barely moving.

After several hours, it quieted down. I was shivering and afraid to go outside in my uniform. I looked around and then I saw the dress. It was hanging on a line — a heavy wool, maroon knit dress. I felt as if God's hand had come down and said, "You will be safe." And I took it.

We slipped out into the night and saw an old German guard with a machine gun — a Wehrmacht soldier, not SS. All of a sudden, a fat woman came in the courtyard and she started screaming, "*Juden!* Kill them. Kill them!"

The old soldier sent the woman back inside. Then he said to us, "Listen. This is the end of the war. The Americans are on the other side of that bridge. I'll shoot over your heads. Just keep running." We didn't believe him, but we ran. He started shooting, and we kept running.

When we crossed the bridge, we saw the American soldiers sitting on their big tanks, looking like angels. They were so friendly and I could understand everything they said, because my mother had made me study English. One soldier got down and I hugged him. I always told myself that if we were ever liberated, I would kiss the first soldier, but I was too bashful. They gave us cheese and bread, and delicious chocolates. We ate it all.

– Lydia E. Lilienheim

A SURVIVOR RETURNS FROM CAMP KRATZAU

The following morning we traveled further west. It was May 15, 1945. We passed through many small villages with foreign-sounding names like Staufnitz, Alt-Schotau and Bensem. The whole area was extraordinarily beautiful. There were cherry trees in full bloom everywhere we looked. Gorgeous landscapes followed each other in quick succession. From our train window we saw terraced fields stacked like braids against the hills in every variety of green. Behind that there were pine trees.

It was getting cozy in the train compartment. An English doctor and nurse came to ask about our health. Our swollen feet got bandaged and we were given some food. Some of the men had managed to find a stove somehow and soon we were able to cook. We had everything — macaroni, semolina, condensed milk, butter, sugar, even some biscuits. People were singing and there was music.

That afternoon we were given soup by the Americans. Our desire to be home again was getting stronger, but so was our fear. How will everything be after the bombardments we heard about and the mass starvation? Will my husband and children still be alive? Let's not think about it, we thought, and just live in the present, for now.

– Geertje Prins-van Coeverden

LEAVING DACHAU

I go through the gate of the camp showing the pass I was given. I walk slowly for about a kilometer and see a field surrounded with trees, not far from the highway. Lilac trees are flowering. I pluck a leaf of elder and put the stalk in my mouth. I spread my coat under a tree and lie down . Rays of sun filter through the leaves and cast golden spots on the red moss. An ant runs onto my hand. As it comes to the end of my finger, I put another finger there to form a bridge and the ant runs from one to the other. As I drop the ant to the ground, a grasshopper leaps from a stalk just in front of the ant. The stalk is still trembling when a yellow field butterfly comes to rest on its leaf. It stops fluttering its speckled wings and folds them gently together. I feel the warm rays of the sun on my face and inhale the sweet scent of the lilacs. How good it is to be alive! The past is only a horrible dream from which I have awakened. Reality is this moment, the scent of the lilacs, the drifting clouds, the softness of the moss.

– Henry Lilienheim

BIRTH

The first snow has fallen, and everything is white. The pendulum of time moves rhythmically. My wife has borne a child. As I bent by the bed of my little daughter, I did not know whether I loved her. But when she smiled for the first time, my heart was full of sweet feelings.

As I look at her, it seems to me I see my mother, my sister, my little niece; I see a reflection of myself. She has come into the world because I did not perish in the camps, and one generation has given hand to another.

– Henry Lilienheim

If there are Survivors present, the host invites them to tell their stories of liberation.

THE SECOND GENERATION

I stare at the photographs displayed all over my bedroom. There, my mother holds a bouquet of white lilies. I marvel at her elegance, at the coy, confident smile whose reality I never witnessed, murdered in a land of nightmares. She did not tell her story too often.

In her last letter she wrote, "All my children are happy. I shall die with a feeling of accomplishment." Of course it isn't true: if it were, I would not understand the lack of bitterness.... As I gaze at the photograph on the night table by my bedside, she smiles, still beautiful, a mother, a wife, a victim of her times, and I love her, I love her, I love her.

– Liliane Richman

We have learned from our parents' tragic experiences that the greatest crime is indifference to the suffering of others. Because of who we are, we may never be passive or allow others to be passive in the face of anti-Semitism or any other form of racial, ethnic or religious hatred, for we know only too well that the ultimate consequence of apathy and silence was embodied forever in the flames of Auschwitz and the mass graves of Bergen-Belsen.

– Menachem Z. Rosensaft

The voices that echo in Dachau can be heard by anyone who listens, not just children of Survivors, but a whole generation that followed and all our children to come.

By facing our history we can begin to understand the forces that allowed the Holocaust to happen; and in its shadow we can begin to create a world rich in meaning and tolerance for everyone.

– Irene Lilienheim Angelico

THE THIRD GENERATION

Dear Zaide,

This is a letter that I cannot send to you through normal channels. I hope you are aware of its contents.

I am your great-grandson. I was born twenty-nine years after you were murdered in Auschwitz. I have just returned from a journey to that site. I walked under the words *"Arbeit Macht Frei"* where you walked. I sat in the barracks where you sat. I stood in the gas chamber where you stood. I touched the oven where your body was cremated.

I have since spent many sleepless nights tortured by thoughts of your pain, panic and torment, during your days in Auschwitz, the last days of your life. What did you know? Did you know the impending doom of your wife, and many of your children and grandchildren?

In your last days I pray that you believed that your beloved Judaism would not also die. I hope you could see that there would be a bright future — that one day, a young man who would know of you as one of his forefathers would return to the place of horror. I was there with 3,500 other young, strong, beautiful, hearty, free Jews. I hope we represented all the Jews all over the world. Although most of the Jews are free to observe their faith, many still are not. We all know that we must dedicate ourselves to their freedom. We will never allow what happened to you to happen again.

We left Auschwitz. In a few short hours we arrived in Israel. I kissed the ground. We danced the hora. We thought of the six million martyrs who died…. [Now], Jews have an independent homeland.

Zaide, though we never have met, I feel you inside me, more so now than ever before. I feel you have given me so much. I keep your spirit alive by keeping your love of Judaism alive, in my love of Judaism.

Zaide, I love you.

> – Jason Stern

If there are children or grandchildren of Survivors present, the host can encourage them to describe what the legacy means to them. They then all stand and say:

THE ACCEPTANCE

WE ACCEPT the obligation of this legacy.

WE ARE the first generation born after the darkness. Through our parents' memories, words and silence, we are linked to that annihilated Jewish existence whose echoes permeate our consciousness.

WE DEDICATE this pledge to you, our parents, who suffered and survived;

TO OUR GRANDPARENTS, who perished in the flames;

TO OUR VANISHED BROTHERS AND SISTERS, more than one million Jewish children, so brutally murdered;

TO ALL SIX MILLION whose unyielding spiritual and physical resistance, even in the camps and ghettos, exemplifies our people's commitment to life.

WE PLEDGE to remember!

WE SHALL TEACH our children to preserve forever that uprooted Jewish spirit which could not be destroyed.

WE SHALL TELL the world of the depths to which humanity can sink, and the heights which were attained, even in hell itself.

WE SHALL FIGHT anti-Semitism and all forms of racial hatred by our dedication to freedom throughout the world.

WE AFFIRM our commitment to the State of Israel and to the furtherance of Jewish life in our homeland.

WE PLEDGE ourselves to the oneness of the Jewish people.

WE ARE YOUR CHILDREN! WE ARE HERE!

Be seated.

RIGHTEOUS GENTILES

Yad Vashem has recognized nearly 24,000 Righteous Gentiles who saved Jews in the Holocaust, at the risk of being shot or sent to the concentration camps themselves. They include, among others, over 6,000 Poles, over 5,000 Dutch, over 3,000 French, over 2,000 Ukranians, 1,600 Belgians, 69 Albanian Muslims, Pope John XXIII, the Danish Underground, the German industrialist Oskar Schindler, the Swede Raoul Wallenberg, Japan's Chiune Sugihara, Portugal's Aristides de Sousa Mendes, Britain's Sir Nicholas Winton, who saved Jewish children, and the Pole Jan Karski, who testified to the Western Allies about the massacres of Polish Jews. And there are many others, like Mrs. Bukowska of the Ukraine, who sheltered Leah, a nine-year-old child survivor of the Romanian transportations from Transnistria in the fall of 1941.

The trees have no conventional beauty. They have that wind-blasted look, stark against the blinding sun. Each one has a name pegged to it, a person's name. No Gentile can visit Yad Vashem without feeling a sense of shame and remorse. But in an act of reconciliation, the Israelis have called the path to the museum the Avenue of the Righteous Among the Nations, and they have planted a tree for every non-Jew who helped. When an overwhelming force was bent on their destruction, a few people reached out to help them … a few exercised their personal freedom in actions that reached into the core of our humanity. And their actions are acknowledged in these trees. And to me no building, statue or obelisk could be as powerful and moving as these stunted but living trees.

– Bottleblondsurfer

Whoever saves one life, saves the world entire.

– Jerusalem Talmud, Sanhedrin 4:8

THE FOURTH CUP
Let us raise this cup to love and peace for all humanity.

Baruch atah adonai, eloheinu melech ha'olam,
boreh pri hagafen.

בָּרוּךְ אַתָּה יְיָ אֱלֹהֵינוּ מֶלֶךְ הָעוֹלָם,
בּוֹרֵא פְּרִי הַגָּפֶן.

They shall beat their swords into ploughshares, and their spears into pruning hooks. Nation shall not lift up sword against nation, nor shall they learn war any more.

    – Isaiah 2:4

LO YISA GOY

Lo yisa goy el goy cherev
lo yilmedu od milchama

} *4 times*

לֹא יִשָּׂא גוֹי

4 פעמים { לֹא יִשָּׂא גוֹי אֶל גוֹי חֶרֶב
לֹא יִלְמְדוּ עוֹד מִלְחָמָה

Nation shall not lift up sword against nation,
nor shall they learn war any more

    – Music by Linda Hirschhorn, lyrics from Isaiah 2:4

DOWN BY THE RIVERSIDE

I'm gonna lay down my sword and shield
down by the riverside, down by the riverside,
down by the riverside.
I'm gonna lay down my sword and shield
down by the riverside.
down by the riverside.

I ain't gonna study war no more,
I ain't gonna study war no more,
I ain't gonna study war no more.

} *2 times*

    – Spiritual

Peace is not a signature endorsing written lines. It is a new writing of history.
Peace is not a contest in trumpeting for it, only to defend any passions
or to conceal any ambitions.
Peace, in its essence, is a giant struggle against passions and ambitions.

To the mother who has lost her son;
To the wife who has been widowed;
To the son who has lost his brother and his father;
To all the war casualties;
Fill the earth and the skies with the hymns of peace;
Fill every heart with hopes for peace;
Let the song be a living blossoming reality;
Let hope be a code of conduct and endeavour;
And the will of people form the will of God.

Peace be upon you.

    – Anwar Sadat

The next song *Oseh Shalom* is probably the best known Jewish prayer for peace. The text recalls the closing lines of the Mourner's Kaddish.

OSEH SHALOM

עֹשֶׂה שָׁלוֹם

Oseh shalom bimromav
hu ya'aseh shalom aleinu
ve'al kol yisrael
ve'imru, imru amen

2 times

2 פעמים

עֹשֶׂה שָׁלוֹם בִּמְרוֹמָיו
הוּא יַעֲשֶׂה שָׁלוֹם עָלֵינוּ
וְעַל כָּל יִשְׂרָאֵל
וְאִמְרוּ. אִמְרוּ אָמֵן

Ya'aseh shalom, ya'aseh shalom
shalom aleinu ve'al kol yisrael

2 times

2 פעמים

יַעֲשֶׂה שָׁלוֹם. יַעֲשֶׂה שָׁלוֹם
שָׁלוֹם עָלֵינוּ וְעַל כָּל יִשְׂרָאֵל

May He who makes peace in the heavens,
grant peace to us, to all Israel,
and to all the inhabitants of the world.
And let us say, Amen.

    – Music by Nurit Hirsh, lyrics from Job 25:2 and the Siddur

And there is hope for peace.

A twelve-year-old girl in a shelter in the Hula Valley wrote this poem for peace:
Come peace to all the world
Come peace to all the people
Come peace on dove wings
Come peace to every country
Boys and girls are awaiting you
Come peace … please come peace.

– Anonymous

SACHAKI

Go ahead, make fun of my dreams,
I'm the one who enjoys the telling,
laugh at me for believing in mankind,
for still believing in you, my dear.

My soul still longs for freedom —
I haven't sold it for a Golden Calf,
for I still believe both in mankind,
and the strength of the human spirit.

I also believe in the future
though it keeps itself far from today,
Indeed a day will come bringing peace
A Blessing from nation to nation.

– S. Tchernichovsky, translated by Ari Snyder

Make love, not war.

– John Lennon

The host and hostess take each other's hands and everyone dances around the table

DODI LI

דודי לי

Dodi li va'ani lo haro'e bashoshanim	} *2 times*	2 פעמים { דוֹדִי לִי וַאֲנִי לוֹ הָרוֹעֶה בַּשׁוֹשַׁנִים
Mi zot ola min hamidbar mi zot ola	} *2 times*	2 פעמים { מִי זֹאת עוֹלָה מִן הַמִּדְבָּר מִי זֹאת עוֹלָה
Dodi li va'ani lo haro'e bashoshanim	} *2 times*	2 פעמים { דוֹדִי לִי וַאֲנִי לוֹ הָרוֹעֶה בַּשׁוֹשַׁנִים
Libavtini achoti kala levavtini kala	} *2 times*	2 פעמים { לִבַּבְתִּינִי אֲחוֹתִי כַּלָּה לִבַּבְתִּינִי כַּלָּה
Dodi li va'ani lo haro'e bashoshanim	} *2 times*	2 פעמים { דוֹדִי לִי וַאֲנִי לוֹ הָרוֹעֶה בַּשׁוֹשַׁנִים
Uri tzafon uvo'i teiman Uri tzafon uvo'i teiman		עוּרִי צָפוֹן וּבוֹאִי תֵּימָן עוּרִי צָפוֹן וּבוֹאִי תֵּימָן
Dodi li va'ani lo haro'e bashoshanim	} *2 times*	2 פעמים { דוֹדִי לִי וַאֲנִי לוֹ הָרוֹעֶה בַּשׁוֹשַׁנִים

My beloved is mine and I am his,
the shepherd among the lilies.

Who is this woman coming from the desert?
Who is she, rising up?

My beloved is mine and I am his,
the shepherd among the lilies.

You have captured my heart, my sister, my bride,
you have captured my heart, my bride.

My beloved is mine and I am his,
the shepherd among the lilies.

Awaken, north wind, and come,
southern wind that blows from Yemen.

My beloved is mine and I am his,
the shepherd among the lilies.

– Music by Nira Chen, lyrics from Song of Songs, 3:6, 4:9, 4:16

LESHANA HABA'AH B'YERUSHALAYIM

לַשָּׁנָה הַבָּאָה בִּירוּשָׁלַיִם

Leshana haba'ah b'yerushalayim
Leshana haba'ah b'yerushalayim

לַשָּׁנָה הַבָּאָה בִּירוּשָׁלַיִם
לַשָּׁנָה הַבָּאָה בִּירוּשָׁלַיִם

Leshana haba'ah b'yerushalayim
Leshana haba'ah b'yerushalayim habenuyah.

לַשָּׁנָה הַבָּאָה בִּירוּשָׁלַיִם
לַשָּׁנָה הַבָּאָה בִּירוּשָׁלַיִם הַבְּנוּיָה.

Next Year in Jerusalem!

– Passover Haggadah

As we sing, everyone is invited to dance.

YISMECHU HASHAMAYIM

יִשְׂמְחוּ הַשָּׁמַיִם

Yismechu hashamayim, yismechu hashamayim
Yismechu hashamayim, vetagel kol ha'aretz
Yir'am hayam, yir'am hayam
Yir'am hayam umelo'o
Yir'am hayam, yir'am hayam
Yir'am hayam umelo'o

יִשְׂמְחוּ הַשָּׁמַיִם. יִשְׂמְחוּ הַשָּׁמַיִם
יִשְׂמְחוּ הַשָּׁמַיִם וְתָגֵל הָאָרֶץ
יִרְעַם הַיָּם. יִרְעַם הַיָּם
יִרְעַם הַיָּם וּמְלֹאוֹ
יִרְעַם הַיָּם. יִרְעַם הַיָּם
יִרְעַם הַיָּם וּמְלֹאוֹ

Let the heavens rejoice, and let the whole earth be glad!
Let the sea roar in all its fullness.

– Music by Akiva Nof, lyrics from Psalm 96.11

As we come to the end of our Third Seder, we wish for peace in Israel and all around the world. Yitzhak Rabin sang this song for peace at a rally just before he was shot. It has become the Israeli peace anthem.

שִׁיר לַשָּׁלוֹם

תְּנוּ לַשֶּׁמֶשׁ לַעֲלוֹת
לַבּוֹקֶר לְהָאִיר,
הַזַּכָּה שֶׁבַּתְּפִילוֹת
אוֹתָנוּ לֹא תַחְזִיר.

מִי אֲשֶׁר כָּבָה נֵרוֹ
וּבֶעָפָר נִטְמַן,
בְּכִי מַר לֹא יְעִירוֹ
לֹא יַחְזִירוֹ לְכָאן.

אִישׁ אוֹתָנוּ לֹא יָשִׁיב
מִבּוֹר תַּחְתִּית אָפֵל, כָּאן לֹא יוֹעִילוּ
לֹא שִׂמְחַת הַנִּיצָחוֹן
וְלֹא שִׁירֵי הַלֵּל.

פזמון:
לָכֵן רַק שִׁירוּ שִׁיר לַשָּׁלוֹם
אַל תִּלְחֲשׁוּ תְּפִילָה
מוּטָב תָּשִׁירוּ שִׁיר לַשָּׁלוֹם
בִּצְעָקָה גְּדוֹלָה!

תְּנוּ לַשֶּׁמֶשׁ לַחֲדוֹר
מִבַּעַד לַפְּרָחִים.
אַל תַּבִּיטוּ לְאָחוֹר,
הַנִּיחוּ לַהוֹלְכִים.

שְׂאוּ עֵינַיִם בְּתִקְוָה,
לֹא דֶרֶךְ כַּוָּנוֹת
שִׁירוּ שִׁיר לָאַהֲבָה
וְלֹא לַמִּלְחָמוֹת.

אַל תַּגִּידוּ יוֹם יָבוֹא -
הָבִיאוּ אֶת הַיּוֹם כִּי לֹא חֲלוֹם הוּא
וּבְכָל הַכִּכָּרוֹת
הָרִיעוּ לַשָּׁלוֹם!

פזמון

SHIR LASHALOM

T'nu lashemesh la'alot
laboker leha'ir
hazakah shebatfilot
otanu lo tachzir.

Mi asher kavah nero
ube'afar nitman
bechi mar lo ya'íro
lo yachziro lechan.

Ish otanu lo yashiv
mibor tachtit afel kan lo yo'ilu
lo simchat hanitzachon
velo shirei halel.

Refrain:
Lachen rak shiru shir lashalom
al tilchashu tefillah
mutav tashiru shir lashlalom
bitze'akah g'dolah!

T'nu lashemesh lachador
miba'ad laprachim
al tabitu le'achor
hanichu laholchim

Se'u einayim betikvah
lo derech kavanot
shiru shir la'ahava
velo lamilchamot

Al tagidu yom yavo
havi'u et hayom, ki lo chalom hu
uvechol hakikarot
hari'u lashalom.

Refrain

Let the sun rise
and give the morning light.
The purest prayer in the Siddur
will not bring us back.

He whose candle was snuffed out
and was buried in the dust,
a bitter cry won't wake him,
won't bring him back.

Nobody can return us
from the dead dark pit.
Here neither the joy of victory
nor songs of praise will help.

Refrain:
So sing only a song for peace,
don't whisper a prayer.

It's better to sing a song for peace,
let shouting fill the air!

Let the sun shine through
to let the flowers grow.
Don't look to the past,
let those who left you go.

Lift your eyes, look up with hope,
not through a rifle's sight,
sing a song, a song of love,
and not a song of war.

Don't tell me the day will come,
but bring us that day, for it is not a dream,
and in every city square
let out a cheer for peace!

Refrain

– Music by Yair Rosenblum, lyrics by Yaakov Rotblit

Just as we have been privileged to hold this Seder, so may we be privileged to carry out its teachings in our actions.

– Henry Granek

Everyone stand for Israel's National Anthem:

HATIKVAH

Kol od balevav penima
nefesh yehudi homia
ulfa'atei mizrach kadima
ayin letzion tzofia

od lo avda tikvateinu
hatikva bat sh'not alpayim
l'hiyot am chofshi be'artzeinu
eretz tzion v'irushalayim

} *2 times*

הַתִּקְוָה

כָּל עוֹד בַּלֵּבָב פְּנִימָה
נֶפֶשׁ יְהוּדִי הוֹמִיָּה
וּלְפַאֲתֵי מִזְרָח קָדִימָה
עַיִן לְצִיּוֹן צוֹפִיָּה

עוֹד לֹא אָבְדָה תִּקְוָתֵנוּ
הַתִּקְוָה בַּת שְׁנוֹת אַלְפַּיִם
לִהְיוֹת עַם חוֹפְשִׁי בְּאַרְצֵנוּ
אֶרֶץ צִיּוֹן וִירוּשָׁלַיִם

{ 2 פעמים

So long as a Jewish soul
still lives within a heart,
and so long as an eye gazes longingly
towards Zion in the far reaches of the East

then the hope is not lost,
the hope of two thousand years,
that we may be a free people in our own land,
the land of Zion and Jerusalem.

– Music by Samuel Cohen, lyrics by Naphtali Herz Imber

ACKNOWLEDGEMENTS

The compilation of this Haggadah evolved over many years and involved the cooperation of many individuals and organizations. Our profound gratitude goes to Henry Granek who originally conceived this Haggadah and led our early Second Generation Seders, and to Simon Dardick of Vehicule Press, who brought his literary, business and personal acumen to the work as it progressed.

Our special thanks go to J.W. Stewart for his profoundly evocative images, to Susan Leviton for her inspiring calligraphy and to Tom Mennier for bringing his formidable creativity and skill to the production of the CD. Thanks to the talented singers and songwriters Ruth Saphir and Geela Rayzel Robinson Raphael who recorded some of the original versions, Burney Lieberman, Bronna Ghita Levy and Joseph Fishman. Peter 'Spanky' Horowitz, Josh Zubot, Christine Ghawi, Adam O'Callaghan, Bill Brooks, Athena Holmes, Katie Young, Akua Carson and Joyce Veeramootoo provided backup singing and music.

Our special appreciation to Ari Snyder, Batia Bettman, Rochelle Rubenstein, Effy Givon, Neil Caplan, Norma Joseph, Myra Giberovitch, Hanna Eliashiv, Bill Surkis, Irina Kondratieva, Kitty Markuze, Shirley Brodt, Julie Guinard and Eddie Paul, as well as the members of Montreal Second Generation, Child Survivors Montreal, Living Testimonies at McGill University, the Montreal Holocaust Memorial Centre, Canadian Jewish Congress and the Jewish Public Library of Montreal. Their suggestions, support and creative input contributed greatly to this Haggadah. Our appreciation also to Avrom Shtern and Bill Brooks for their research into the sources of the prose and music respectively, and to Shy Shalev for setting and editing the Hebrew text.

We are pleased to thank Rabbi Ron Aigen of Congregation Dorshei Emet, Rabbi Leigh Lerner of Temple Emanu-El-Beth Sholom and Rabbi Reuben Poupko of Congregation Beth Israel Beth Aaron for contributing their wisdom to the writing of the Haggadah and for offering a welcoming place to hold The Third Seder.

We are grateful to the Montreal Holocaust Memorial Centre, Canadian Jewish Congress (Quebec Region), the Jewish Community Foundation of Montreal, the Jack Dym Family Foundation and the Tauben Family Foundation for their financial support.

We acknowledge all those whose work we have included and whose insightful and moving contributions will live on in these pages. We have tried to name as many of them as possible. We regret any omissions and welcome information that will help identify these sources.

With admiration and respect, we thank all the Survivors. It is their experience, courage and wisdom that has informed this Haggadah and enriched our lives.

With all our love, we thank our families: our children Toben Neidik and David Markus, who fill us with hope for the future; our partners Abbey Neidik and Françoise de la Cressonnière, who have given so many brilliant suggestions about the many Third Seders we have shared; and our parents, Henry and Lydia Lilienheim, and Nico and Betsy Lindeman, who are our heroes and our greatest inspiration.

– Irene Lilienheim Angelico and Yehudi Lindeman

My parents Eugenia Lydia Turkus and Henry Lilienheim were married by candlelight in Warsaw at the start of the war. Later, they were captured and sent to a series of camps. They were the only ones in their families to survive. After their liberation, my father travelled throughout Europe searching for his wife, but finally it was her letter to the Tracing Office in Munich that led him to her. These photographs and documents are a testimony to my parents' love for each other, their will to live, and their commitment to begin a new life and family far from home.

– Irene Lilienheim Angelico

My mother Bets Lindeman-van Coevorden gave birth to me in March 1938 during the week that the German army marched into Vienna. My first memories are the wailing sounds of the air sirens during the German invasion of Holland in the spring of 1940. I survived in hiding in about fifteen different locations all over Holland. These photographs and documents are a tribute to my mother, whose foresight and determination helped save my life and who luckily found me after the war. They are also a testimony to the dozens of rescuers who endangered their own lives and that of their families so that I might live.

– Yehudi Lindeman

CREDITS

THE BOOK

17 "In the beginning…" is from "Jewish Values in the Post Holocaust Future: A Synopsis," by Elie Wiesel which appeared in Judaism, vol. 16, no. 3, American Jewish Congress, 1967.

17 "Our first celebration…" is adapted from the Passover Haggadah by Henry Granek and Irene Lilienheim Angelico.

18 "The month of spring…" is from Seasons of Our Joy, Summit Books, N.Y., p. 133

21 "Remember the time…" by Albert Memmi appeared in Jewish Liberation Haggada, Aviva Cantor Zuckoff, ed., Jewish Liberation Project, N.Y., 1970

25 "Tonight we gather…", Anti-Defamation League

29 "The birthrate in the DP camps…" Based on the keynote address by Samuel Norich, World Gathering of Jewish Holocaust Survivors, Jerusalem, June 17, 1981. (Published by YIVO Institute of Jewish Research).

30 "Passover 1944: A Prayer for Eating Chametz." Rabbis in the Bergen Belsen concentration camp. A copy of the original handwritten prayer is in the Ghetto Fighters House, Israel.

31 When Rabbi Meir died…". Adapted from "Sota 9.15," The Mishna, translated by Herbert Danby, Oxford University Press, London and Toronto, 1933, pp 305-306. Reprinted by permission of Oxford University Press.

31 "When Kalman the shoemaker…" is from Night Words: A Midrash on the Holocaust by David Roskies, B'nai B'rith Hillel Foundation, Inc. Reprinted by permission of the author.

32 "Passover, 1942" from "A Message from Samuel Bronfman," President, Canadian Jewish Congress, which appeared in The Canadian Jewish Chronicale, April 16, 1943. Reprinted by permission of the Canadian Jewish Congress.

32 "Count by ones…" by Anonymous appeared in David Roskies' Night Words: A Midrash on the Holocaust.

33 "Babi Yar by Yevgeni Yevtushenko; translator unknown.

35 "Dearest Bronia…" from "Letters from the Ghetto" is a source document that appeared in Holocaust Reader, Lucy S. Dawidowicz, ed., Behrman House Inc., N.Y., 1976.

36 "At My Bar Mitzvah—and His" by Rabbi Howard Kahn appeared in Life Lines: A Rabbi Looks at His World, Congregation Beth El, Cherry Hill, N.J., 1995. Reprinted by permission of Sammy Kahn and Congregation Beth El.

40 "It is true…" appeared in Faith After the Holocaust by Eliezer Berkovitz, originally published by Ktav Publishing House, N.Y., 1973.

41 "The Fifth Child" is from The Jewish Way: Living the Holidays by Rabbi Irving Greenberg, Touchstone, N.Y. 1993. Reprinted by permission of Clal, The National Jewish Center for Learning and Leadership, © copyright 2005.

44 "The Legacy" by Elie Wiesel, translated by Menachem Z. Rosensaft, was presented at the Closing Ceremony, World Gathering of Jewish Holocaust Survivors, Jerusalem, June 18, 1981. Reprinted by permission of the American Gathering of Jewish Holocaust Survivors and Their Descendants.

45 "Lydia's Story" appeared in The Aftermath: A Survivor's Odyssey through War-Torn Europe by Henry Lilienheim, DC Books, 1994. Reprinted by permission of Irene Lilienheim Angelico.

46 "Leaving Dachau" appeared in The Aftermath: A Survivor's Odyssey through War-Torn Europe by Henry Lilienheim, DC Books, 1994. Reprinted by permission of Irene Lilienheim Angelico.

47 "Birth" appeared in The Aftermath: A Survivor's Odyssey through War-Torn Europe by Henry Lilienheim, DC Books, 1994. Reprinted by permission of Irene Lilienheim Angelico.

48 "I stare at the photograph…" from "The Family Album" by Liliane Richman appeared in Living After the Holocaust: Reflections by Children Survivors in America, Lucy Y. Steinitz and David M. Szonyi, eds., Bloch Publishing, N.Y., 1975.

48 "We have learned from our parents' tragic…." From "Day of Remembrance" by Menachem Z. Rosensaft was included in the National Holocaust Commemoration, U.S. Memorial Council, Washington, D.C., April 11-13, 1983. Reprinted by permission of the author.

48 "The voices that echo in Dachau…." is from Dark Lullabies, a film by Irene Lilienheim Angelico and Abbey Neidik, © DLI Production and National Film Board of Canada, 1985.

49 "Dear Zaide…" by Jason Stern, appeared in For You Who Died I Must Live On: Reflections on the March of the Living, Eli Rubenstein, ed., Mosaic Press, Oakville, Ontario, 1991.

50 "The Acceptance" was presented at the Closing Ceremony, World Gathering of Jewish Holocaust Survivors, Jerusalem, June 18, 1981. Reprinted by permission of the American Gathering of Jewish Holocaust Survivors and Their Descendants.

51 "The trees have no conventional beauty…" by Bottleblondsurfer appeared in "The Avenue of Righteous Gentiles,"

54 "Peace is not a signature…" is excerpted from a speech by Anwar Sadat delivered in Arabic to the Israeli Knesset, November 20, 1977.

55 "Sachaki" by Shaul Tchernichovsky, translated by Ari Snyder. Reprinted by Permission of Ari Snyder.

59 "Just as we have been privileged…" by Henry Granek appeared in an unpublished version of The Third Seder, Montreal, 1987. Reprinted by permission of the author.

63-64 Images used in the two collages by permission of the authors.

THE CD: Songs for Yom HaShoah

[The Third Seder is published in two editions—one with a CD and one without. These are the credits for the CD]

Produced by Tom Mennier
Co-produced by Yehudi Lindeman and Ruth Saphir
Special assistance: Bill Brooks

Fire and Roses: Music and lyrics by Ruth Saphir and Cedric M. Speyer
Miriam: Music and lyrics by G. Rayzel Robinson Raphael
Singers: Ruth Saphir, G. Rayzel Robinson Raphael, Burney Lieberman, Bronna Ghita Levy and Joseph Fishman.
Backup singing and music: Peter 'Spanky' Horowitz, Josh Zubot, Christine Ghawi, Adam O'Callaghan, Bill Brooks, Athena Holmes, Katie Young, Akua Carson and Joyce Veeramootoo.

All song selections in the accompanying CD are public domain except for the titles that are followed by a "*" symbol on the Song List or otherwise indicated. Permission for the use of these songs has been granted under license by the copyright owners or their authorized representatives.

SONG LIST

Hine Ma Tov
Erets Zavat Chalav (Land of Milk and Honey) *
Zog Maran *
Go down Moses
Miriam Took Her Timbrel Out [See above]
Shtil di Nacht (Schtille di Nacht)
Zog nit Keynmol (Hymn of the Partisans)
Fire and Roses [See above]
Kol Ha olam Kulo (Gesher tsar m'od) *

Ani Ma'amin
Lo Yisa Goy
Down by the Riverside
Oseh Shalom *
Dodi Li *
Leshana Haba'a B'Yerushalayim
Yismechu Hashamayim *
Shir La Shalom *
Hatikvah (National anthem of Israel)

APPENDIX

Hineh Ma Tov

Eretz Zavat Chalav Ud'vash

(unaccompanied)

Miriam

Music and lyrics by
G. Rayzel Robinson Raphael

D.C.

They danced so hard,
they danced so fast,
they danced with movement strong.
Laughed and cried, brought out alive,
they danced until the dawn.

And Miriam took her timbrel out...

Some carrying child,
some baking bread,
weeping as they prayed,
but when they heard that music start
they put their pain away.

Zog Maran

Music by Shmuel Bugatch
Lyrics by Avrom Reisen

Go Down Moses

Negro spiritual

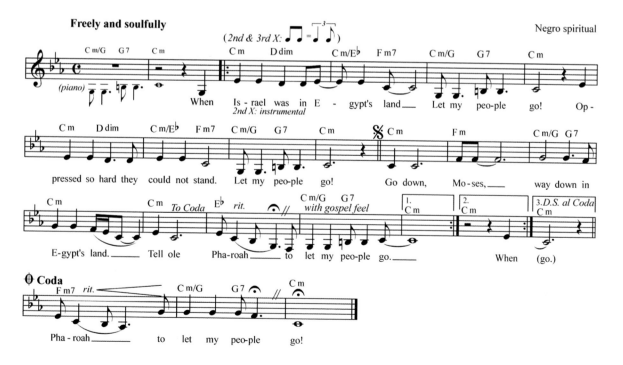

Shtil di Nacht

Music and lyrics by Hirsh Glik

3.

Getsilt, geshosn un getrofn
hot ir kleyninker pistoyl,
an oito a fulinken mit vof'n
farhaltn hot zi mit eyn koyl.

4.

Fartog, fun vald aroysgekroch'n,
mit shney-girlandn oyf di hor,
gemutikt fun kleyninkn nitsoch'n,
far undzer nayem, frayen dor!

Zog Nit Keynmol
(Hymn of the Partisans)

Music and lyrics by Hirsh Glik
Translated by Elliot Palevsky

Alla marcia ♩ = 112

(accordion)

1., 4. Zog nit keyn-mol az du geyst dem lets-tn-
2. Fun gri-nem pal-men-land viz vay-sn land fun
3. Gesh-rib-n iz dos lid mit blut un nit mit

veg, Chotsh him-len blay-e-ne-far-shte-ln-bloy-e teg; Ku-men
shney, mir ku-men on mit und-zer payn, mit und-zer vey. Un vu
blay, s'iz nit keyn lid-l fun a foy-gl oyf der fray; dos hot a

vet noch und-zer oys-ge-benk-te sho, S'vet a poyk ton und-zer trot: "mir zay-nen
gef-aln s'iz a shprits fun und-zer blut, shprot-sen vet dort und-zer gvur-e, und-zer
folk ts'-vish-n fal-n-dik-e vent dos lid ge zung-en mit nag-an-es in di

1, 3, 5, 7. | 2, 4. | 6.
do!" Ku-men do!" D.C. do!" D.S. al Coda
mut. Un vu mut.
hent. dos hot a hent.

4. To zog nit

CODA
do!" sf

— 69 —

Fire & Roses

Music and lyrics by
Ruth Saphir & Cedric M. Speyer

2.
The women hang their washing on the line
voices laughing, chattering like chimes.
How I wish that I could reach back in time
across the fence of history with all I claim as mine.
How I wish that when I tuck my child into bed
she could see their faces, hear their songs instead.

3.

The men are strolling slowly down the street
they stop and chat with old friends that they meet.
How I wish that I could reach back in time
to break bread together, drink a toast to the divine.
How I wish that they could all gather with us here
tell the million stories lost when millions disappeared.

4.

Their souls cry out so loudly to me
in the roaring raging flame of inhumanity.
But I feed them roses, they taste my tears and smile
I will be their comfort for a little while.

(CODA)

Yes, I feed them roses, I give them each a smile
I will be their comfort for awhile.

Kol Ha'olam Kulo

Music by Baruch Chait
Lyrics from Rabbi Nachman of Breslov

Ani Ma'amin

Traditional
Lyrics from Maimonides

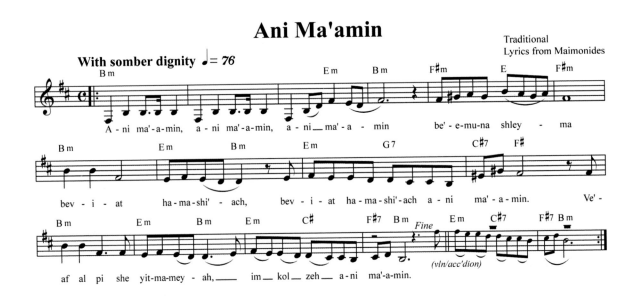

Lo Yisa Goy

Music by Linda Hirschhorn
Lyrics from Isaiah 2:4

Down By The Riverside

Traditional

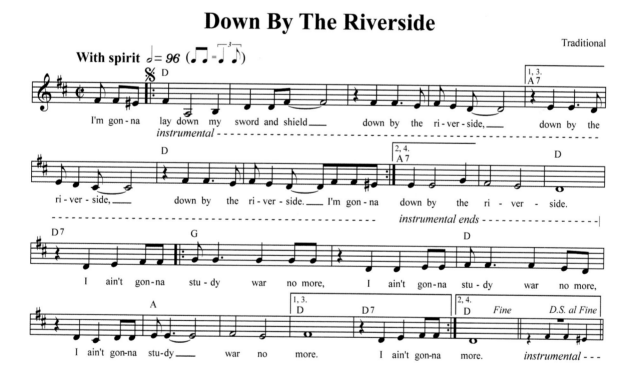

Oseh Shalom

Music by Nurit Hirsh
Lyrics from the Siddur

Dodi Li

Music by Nira Chen
Lyrics from Song of Songs
2:16, 3:6, 4:9, 4:16

Leshana Haba'ah B'yerushalayim

Yismechu Hashamayim

Shir Lashalom

Music by Yair Rosenblum
Lyrics by Yaakov Rotblit

Hatikvah

Music by Samuel Cohen
Lyrics by Naphtali Herz Imber

With dignity

(accordion)

Kol__ od ba-lé-vav p'-ni-ma ne-fesh y'-hu-di ho-mi-ya ul'-fa-a té__miz-rach ka-di-ma a-yin l'-tsi-yon tso-fi-ya od lo av-da tik-va-té-nu ha-tik-va bat shnot al-pa-yim li-yot am chof-shi b'-ar-tsé-nu e-rets tsi-yon y'-ru-sha-la-yim li-yot am chof-shi b'-ar-tsé-nu e-rets tsi-yon y'-ru-sha-la-yim